- Always Supervise Young Children During Scissor Skill Practice
- Use Age Appropriate Scissors With Blunt Tips
- Show Kids How To Properly Hold Scissors And Cut Papers
- Explain That Scissors Are Not Toys And Should Be Used Responsibly

Scissors Skills

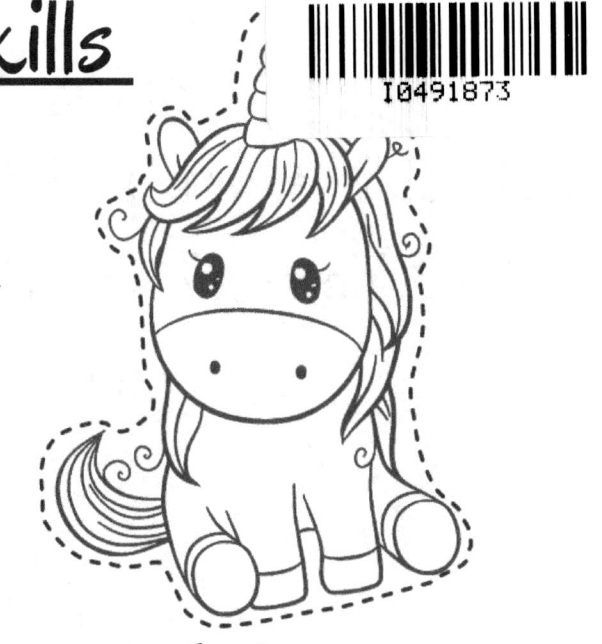

Step 1:
Cut Page out of The Book

Step 2:
Color The Picture

Step 3:
Cut Out Picture Along The Dotted Lines

Step 4:
Paste Picture on Another Sheet or Hong

Step 5:
Paste Picture on Sheet and Color

Thank you for your recent purchase. We hope you love it! If you do, would you consider posting an online review? This helps us to continue providing great products and helps potential buyers to make confident decisions. Thank you in advance for your review and for being a preferred customer.

This Book Belongs To

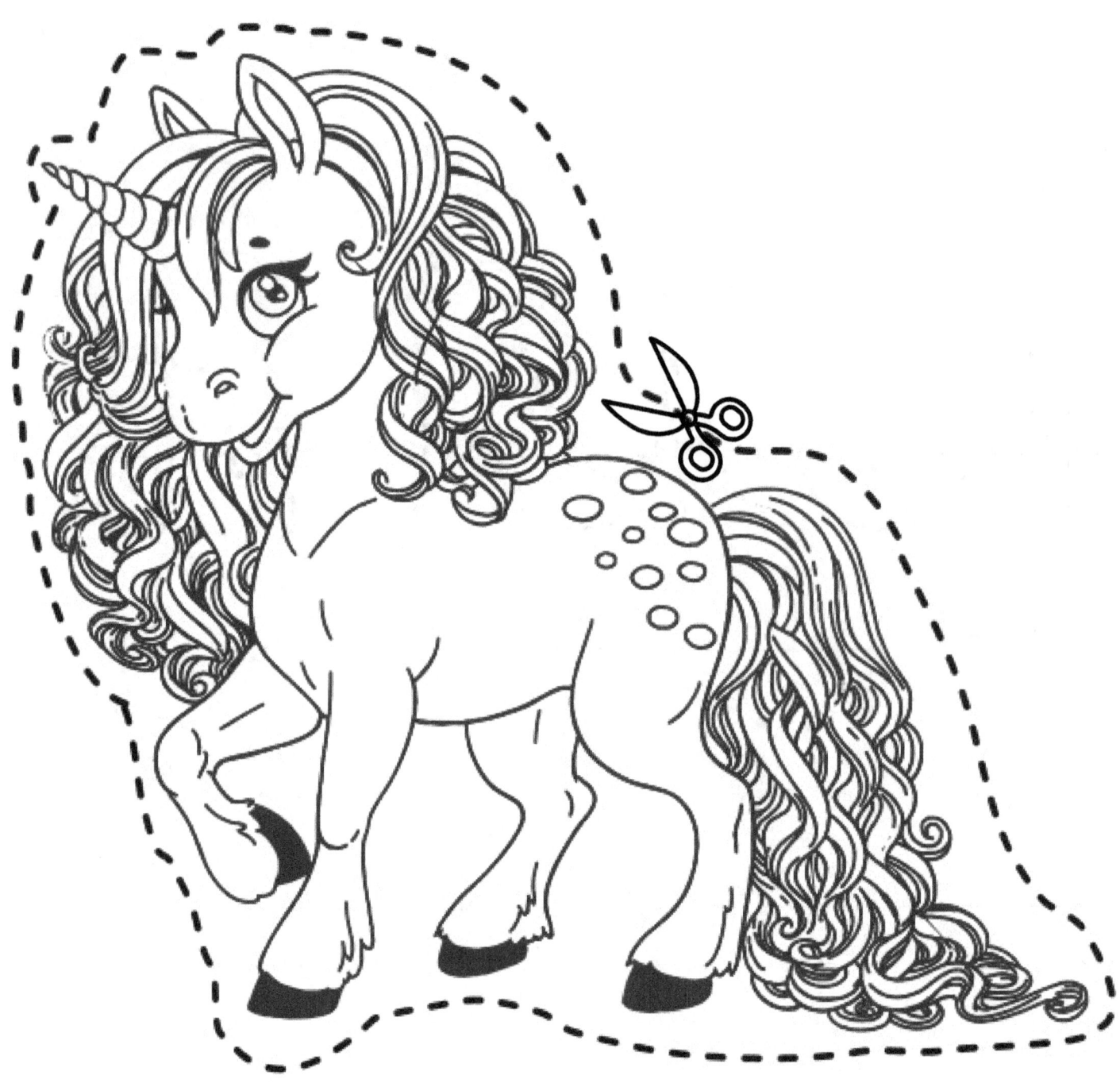

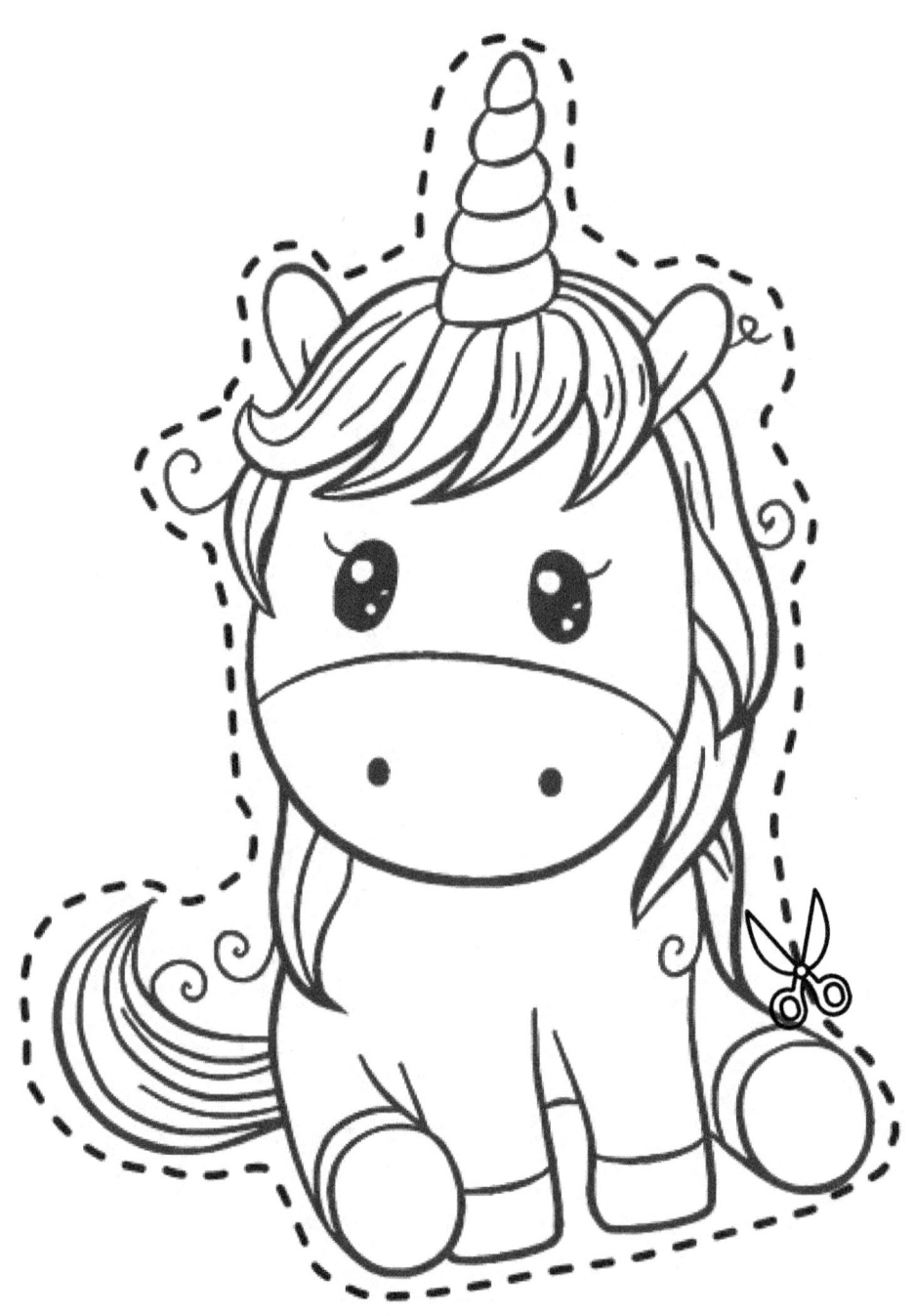

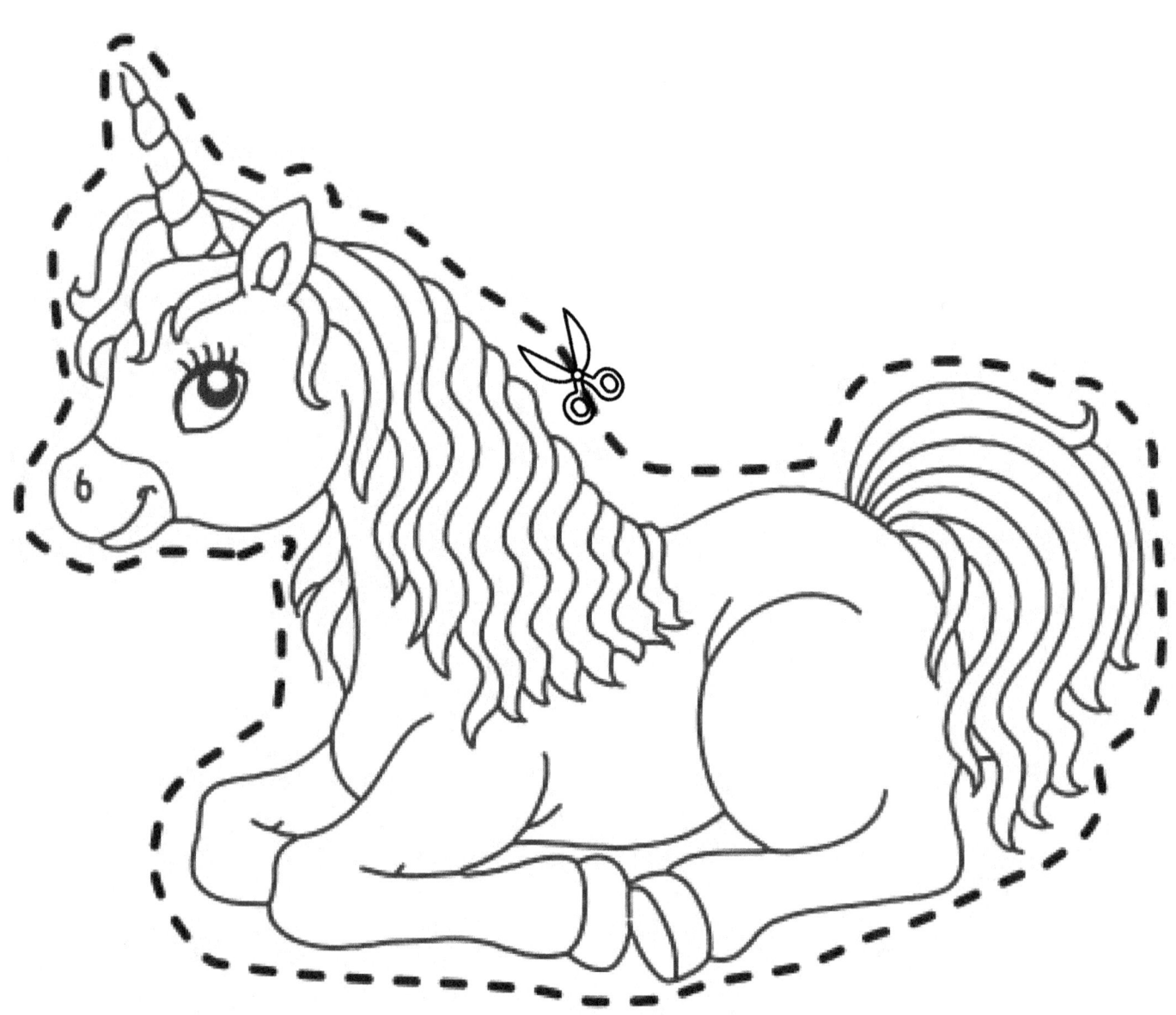

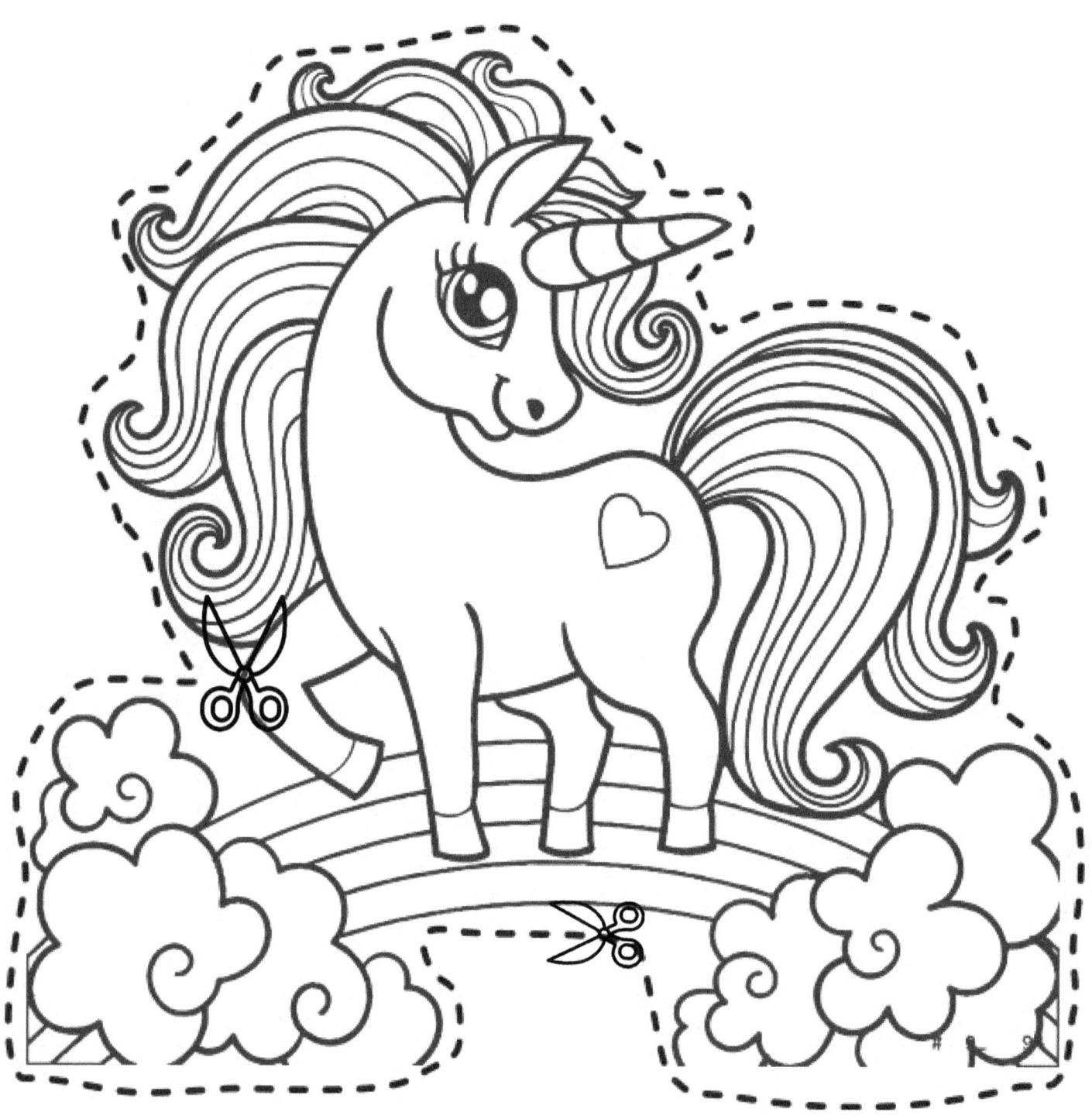

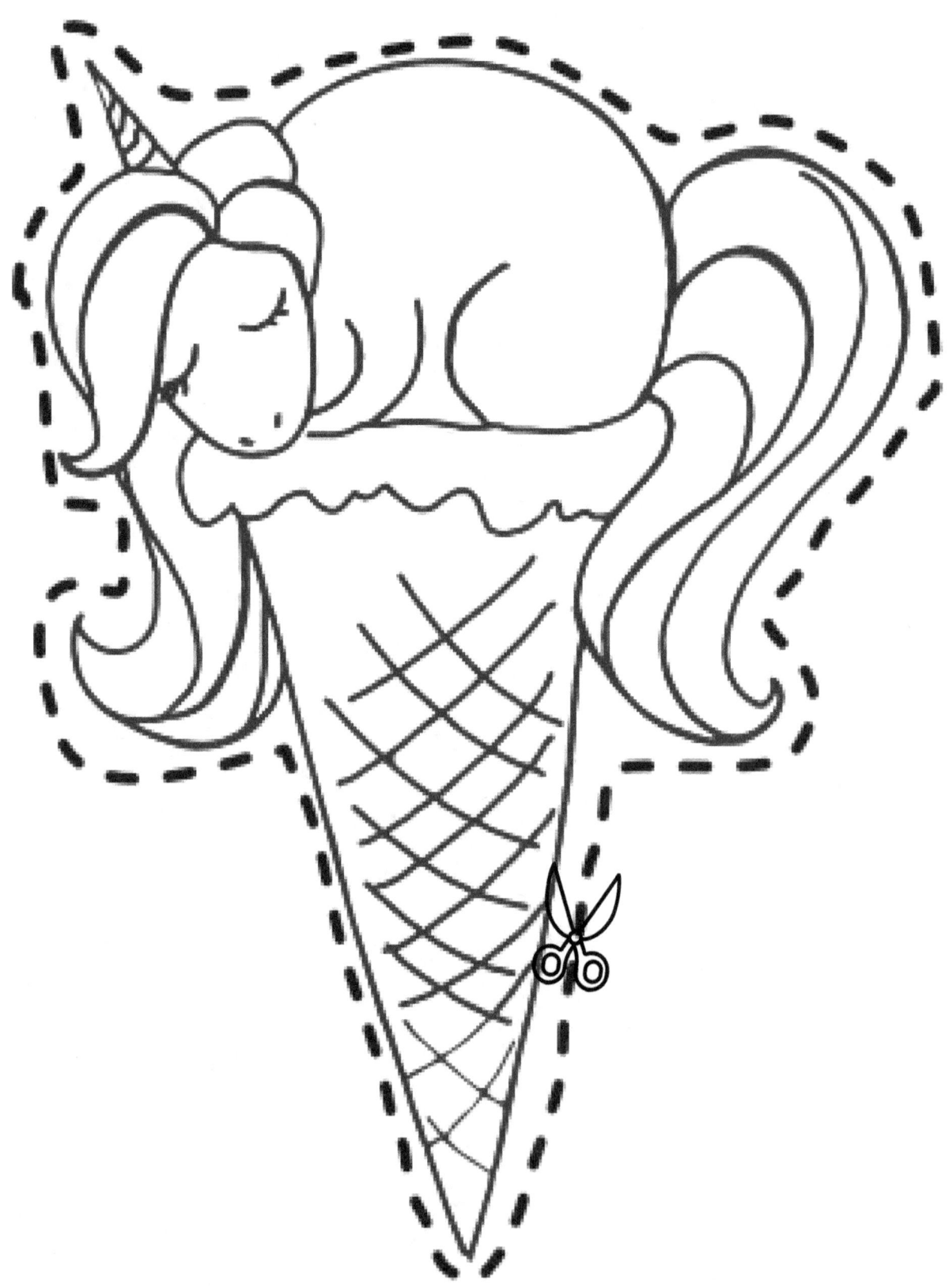

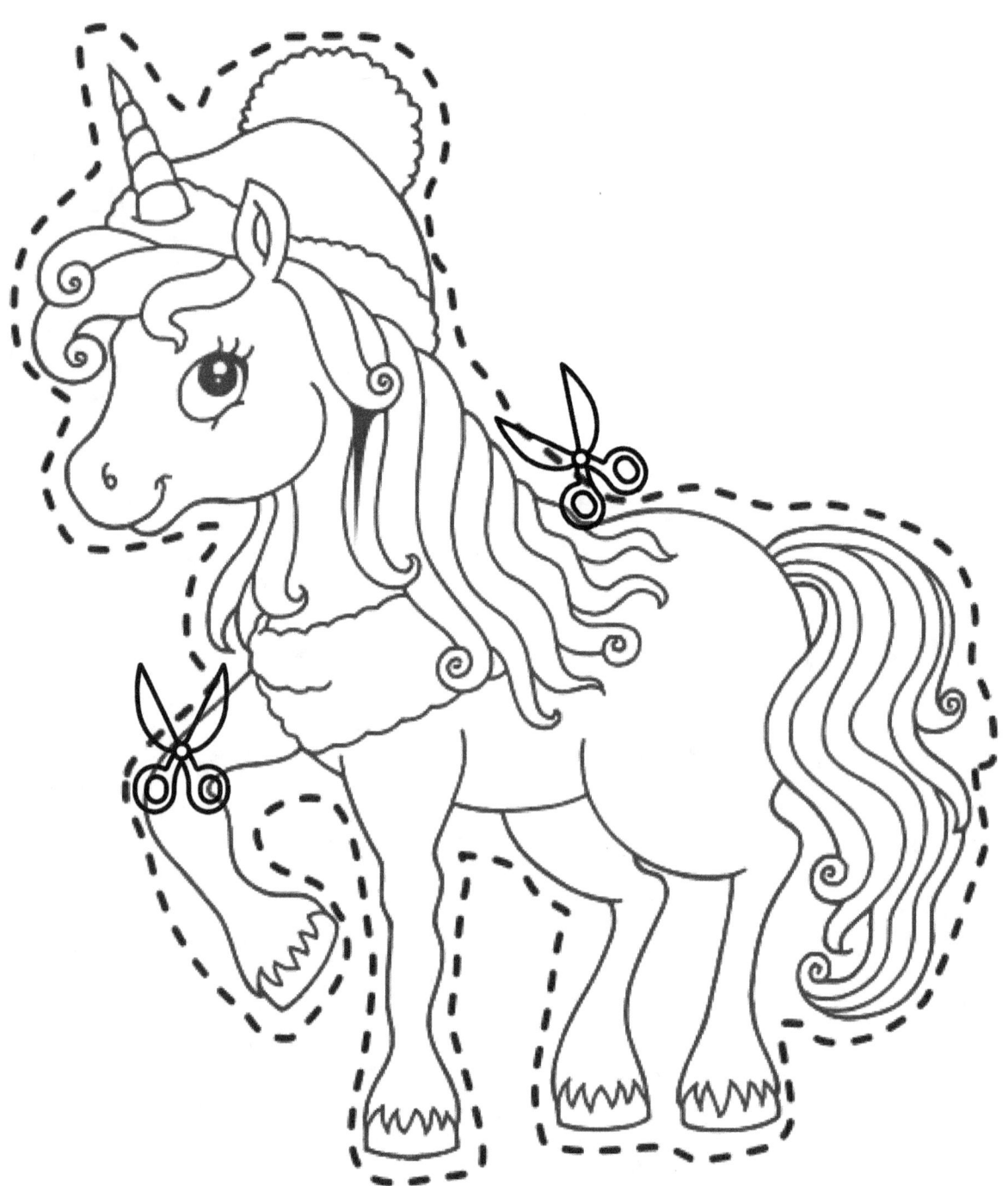

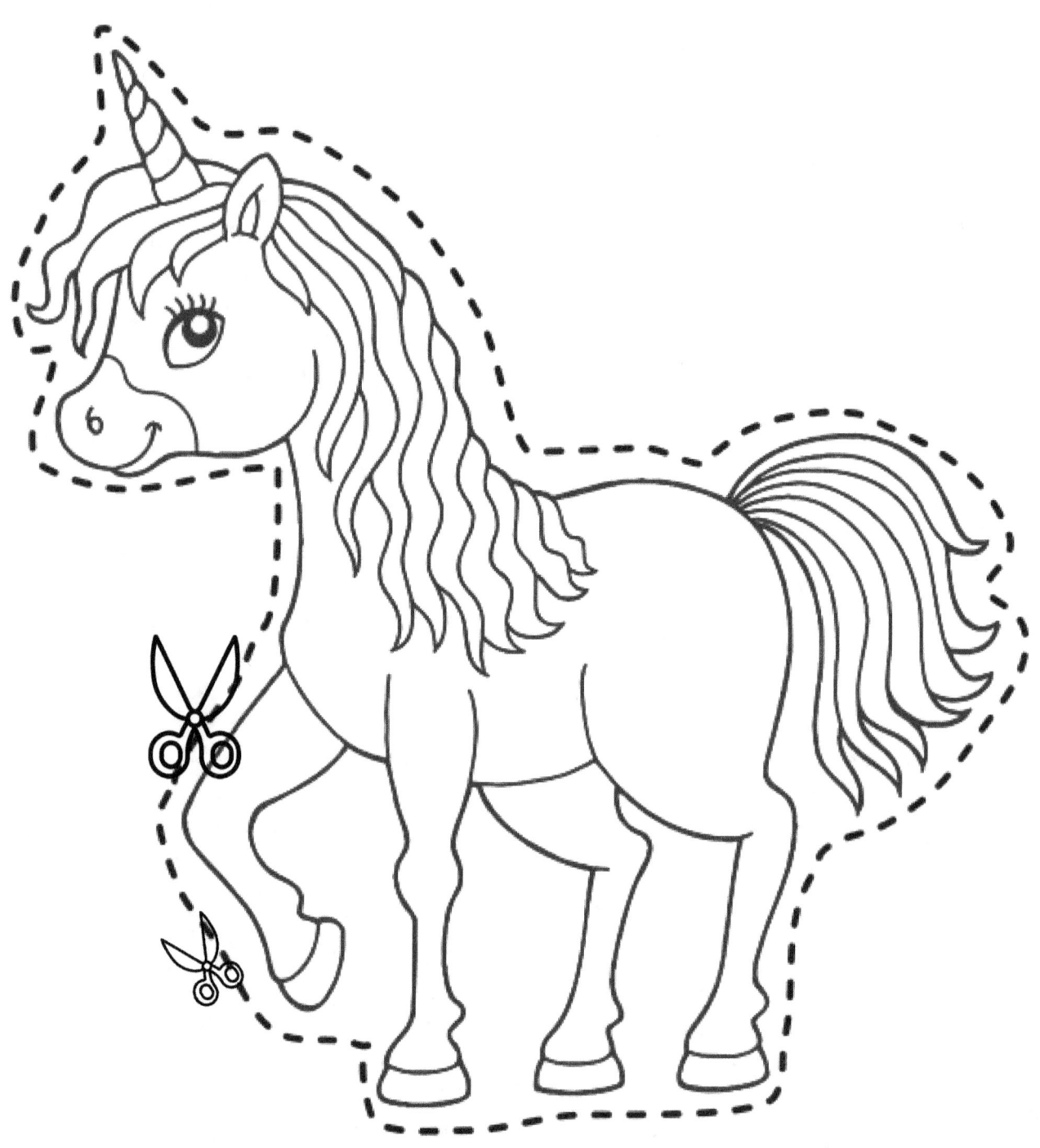

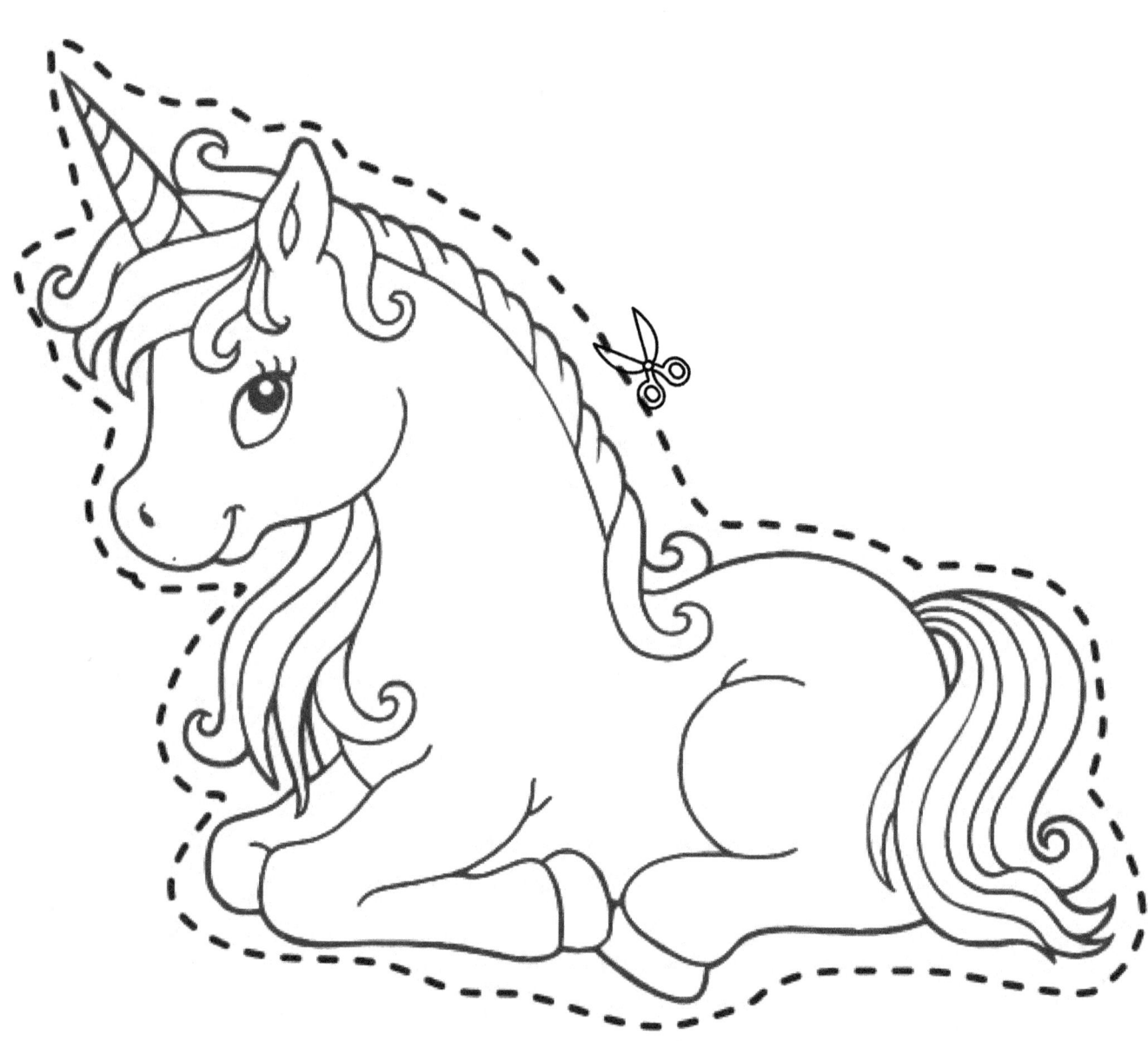

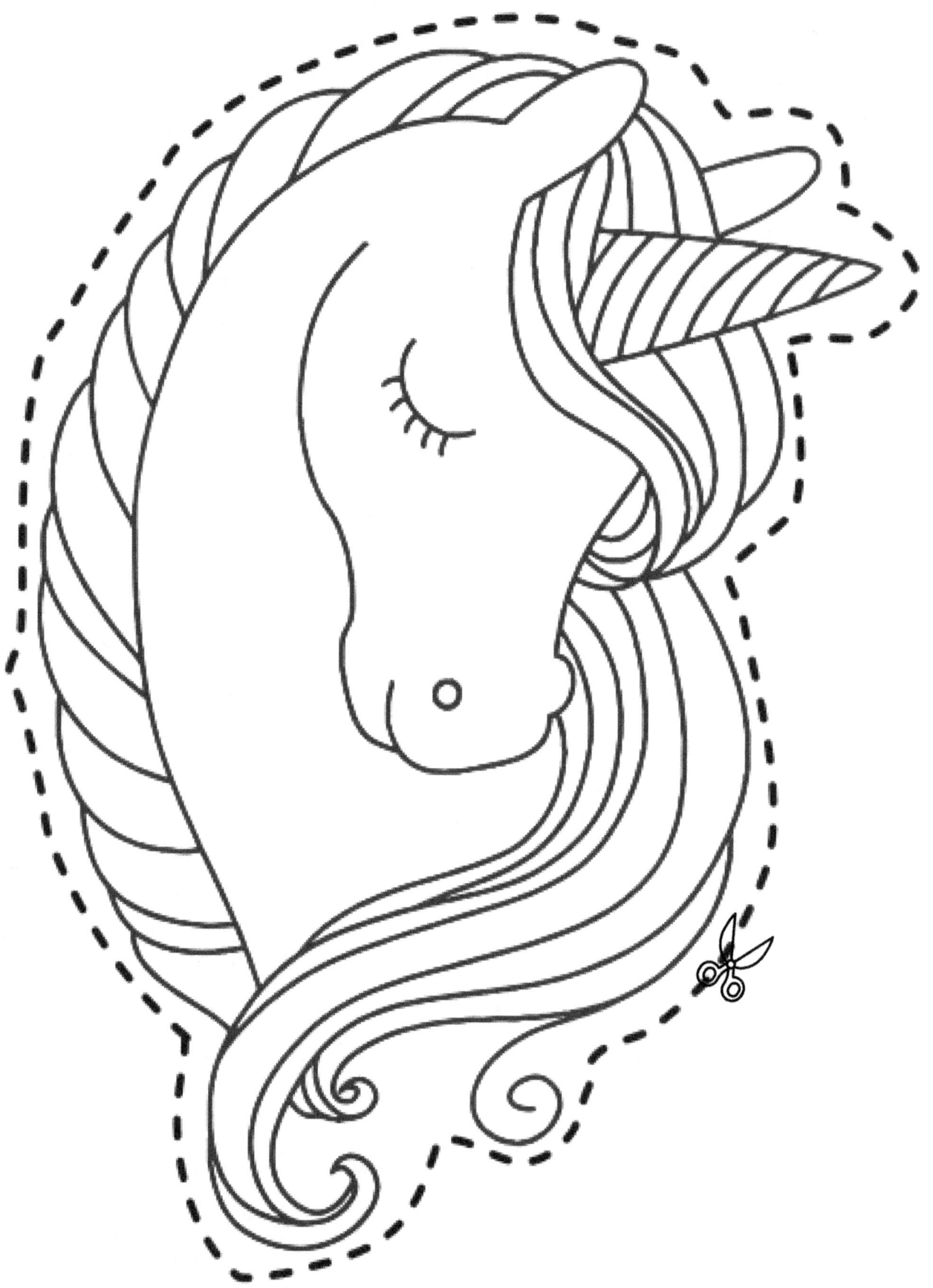

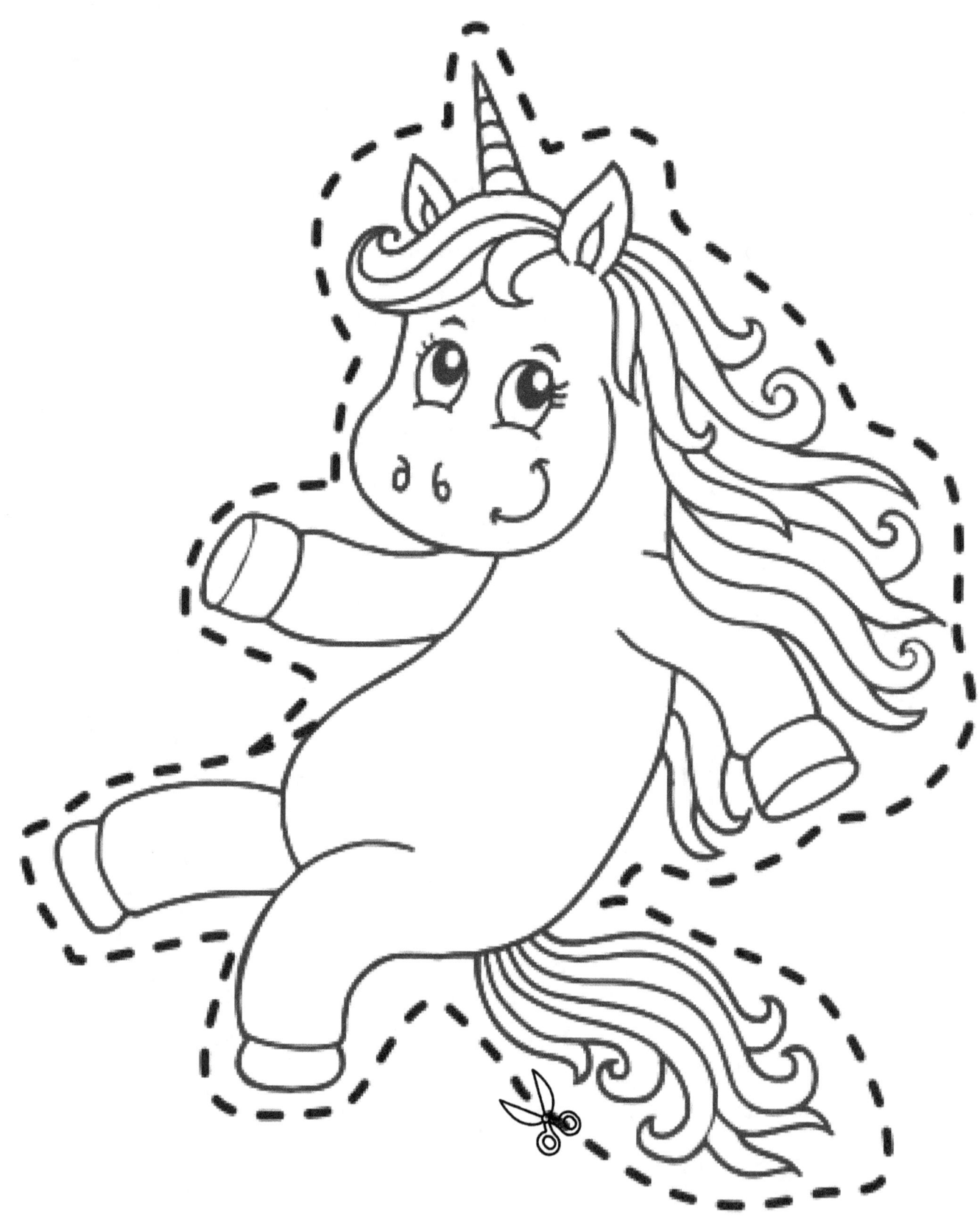

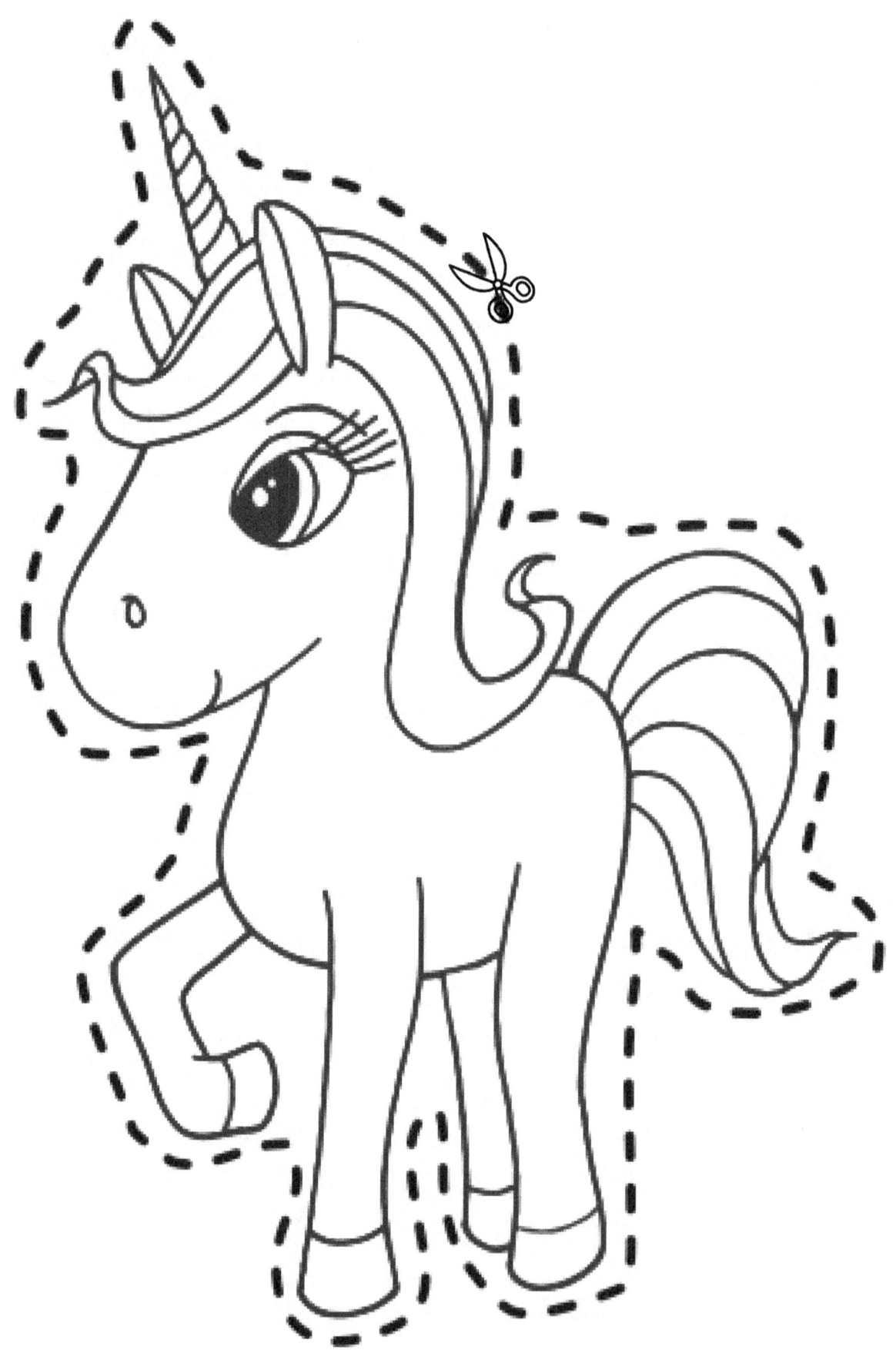

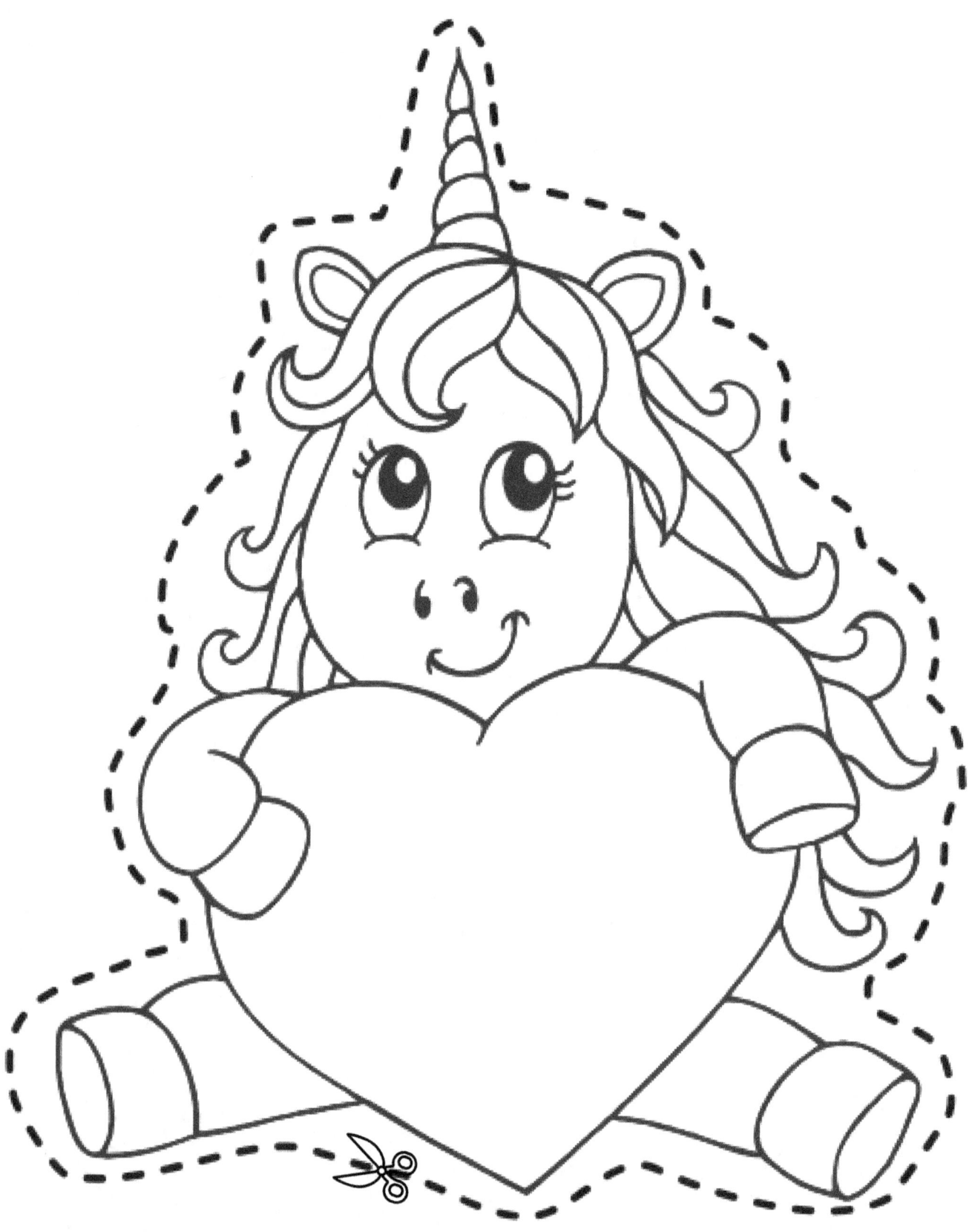

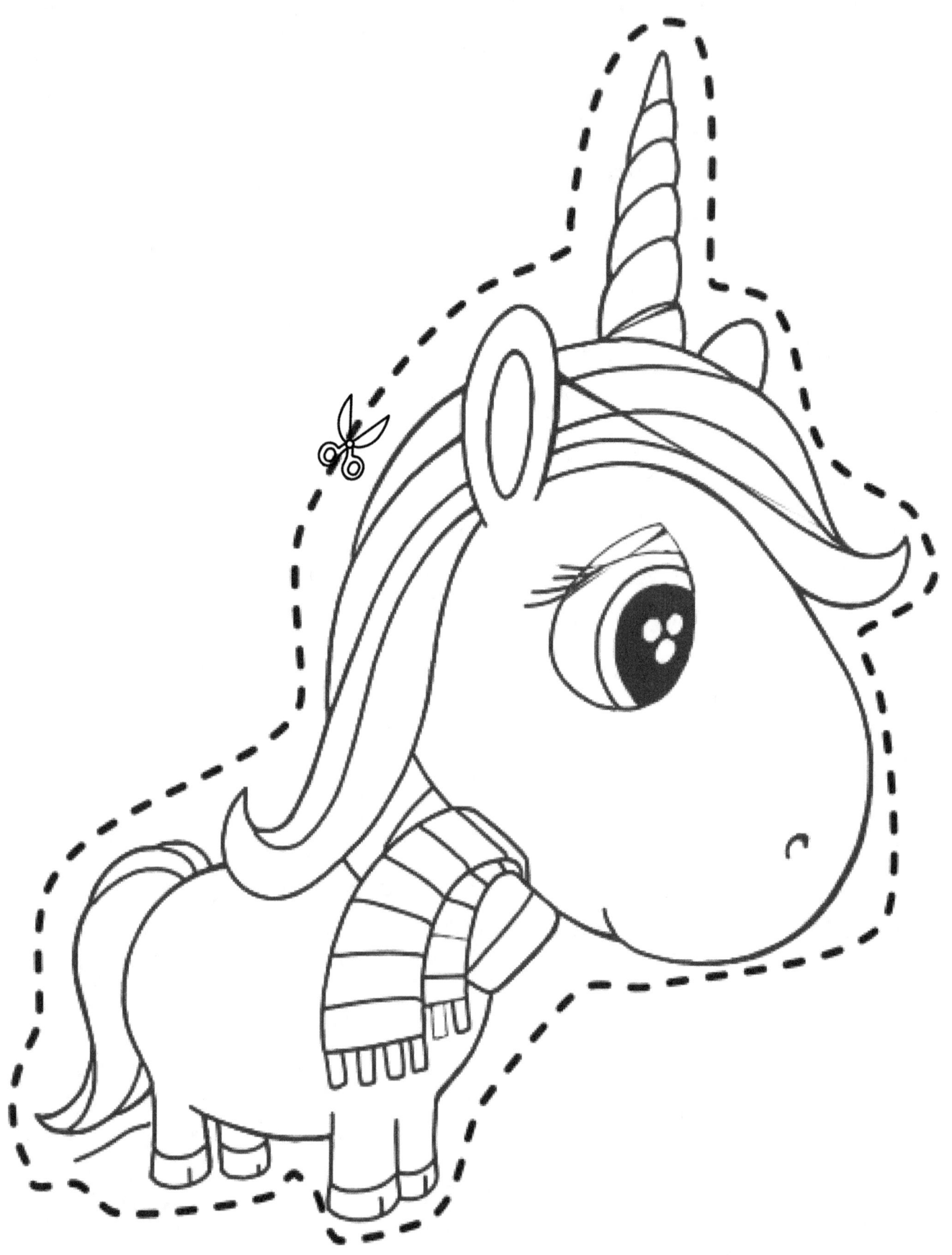

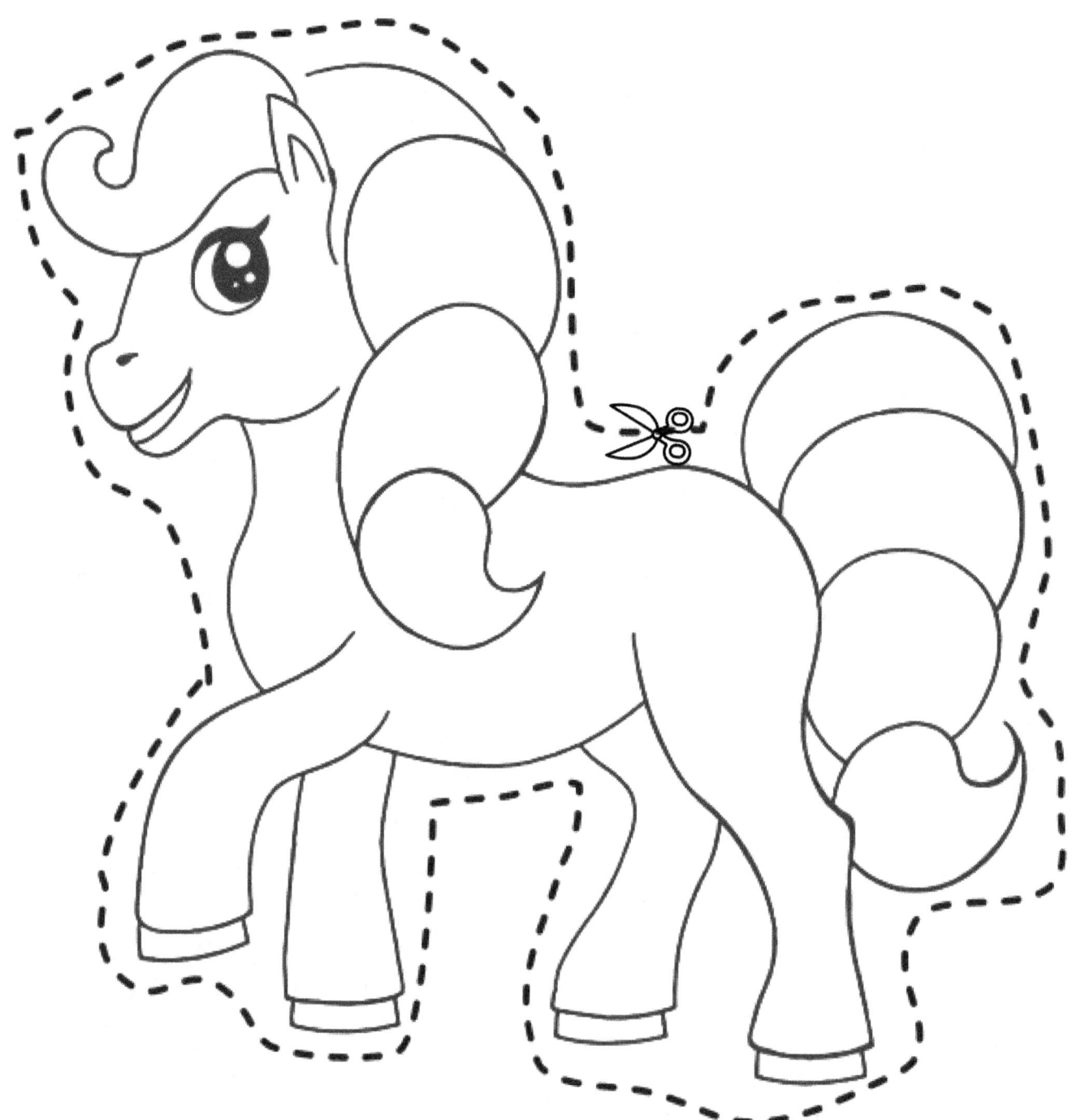

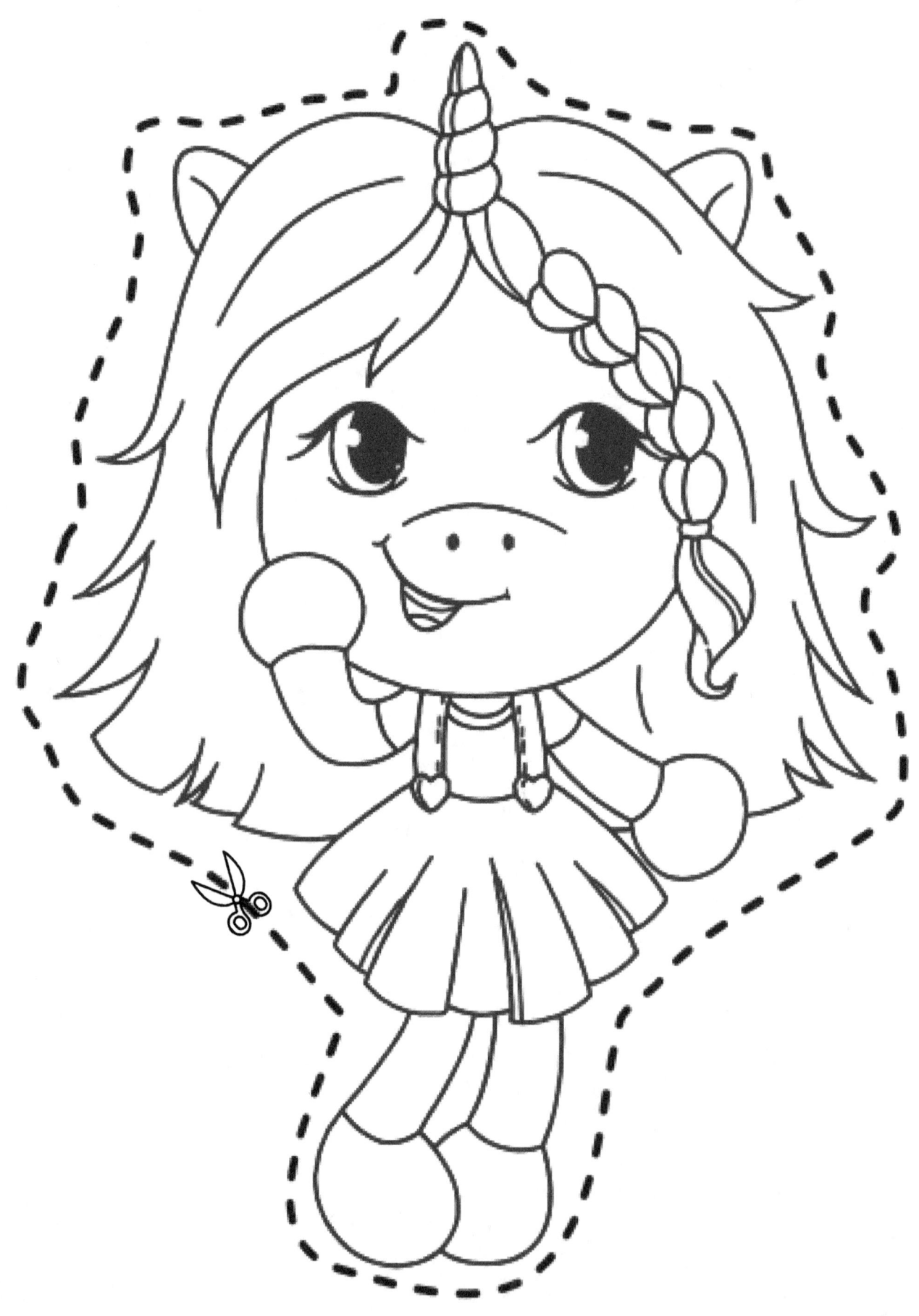

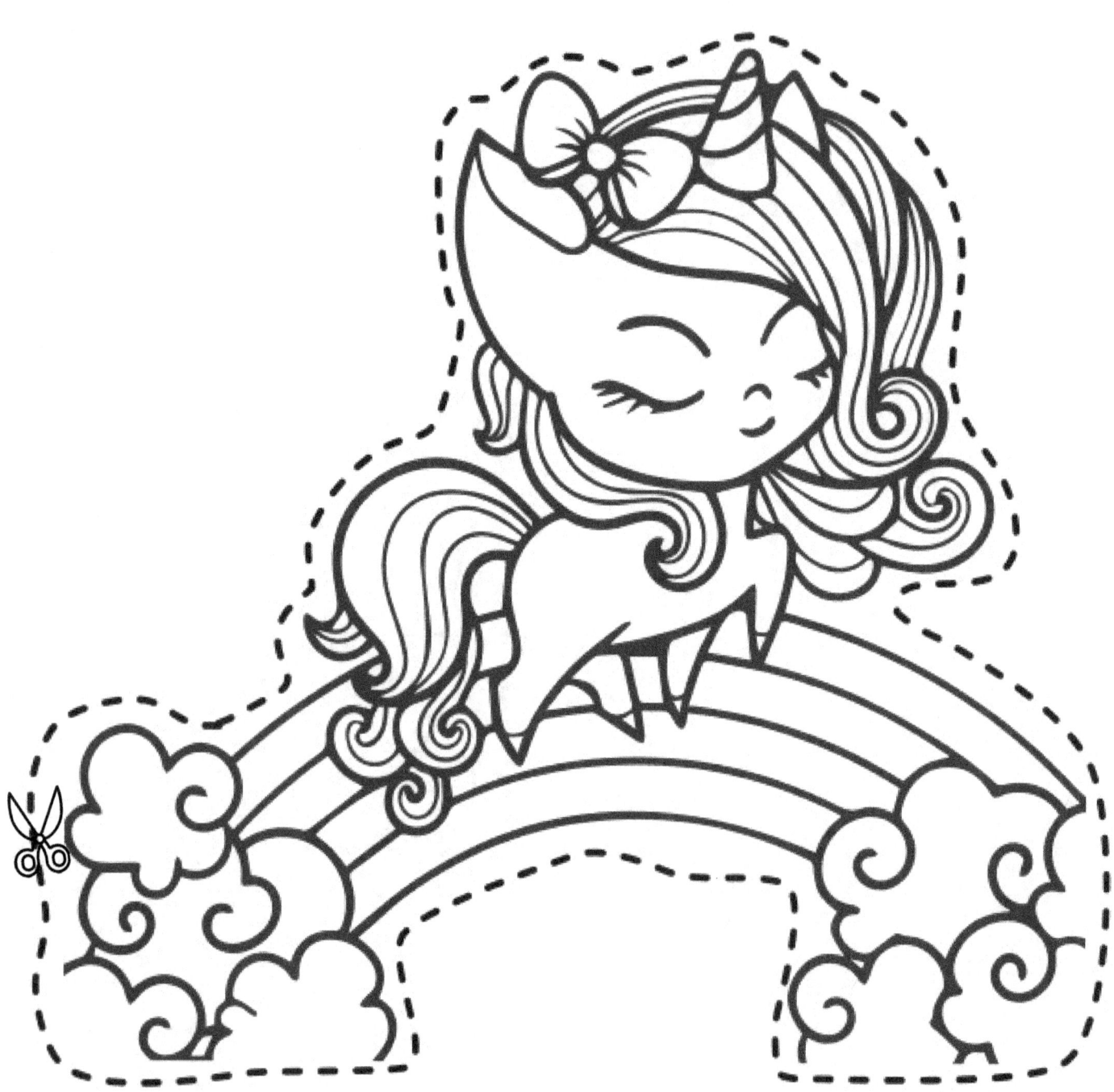

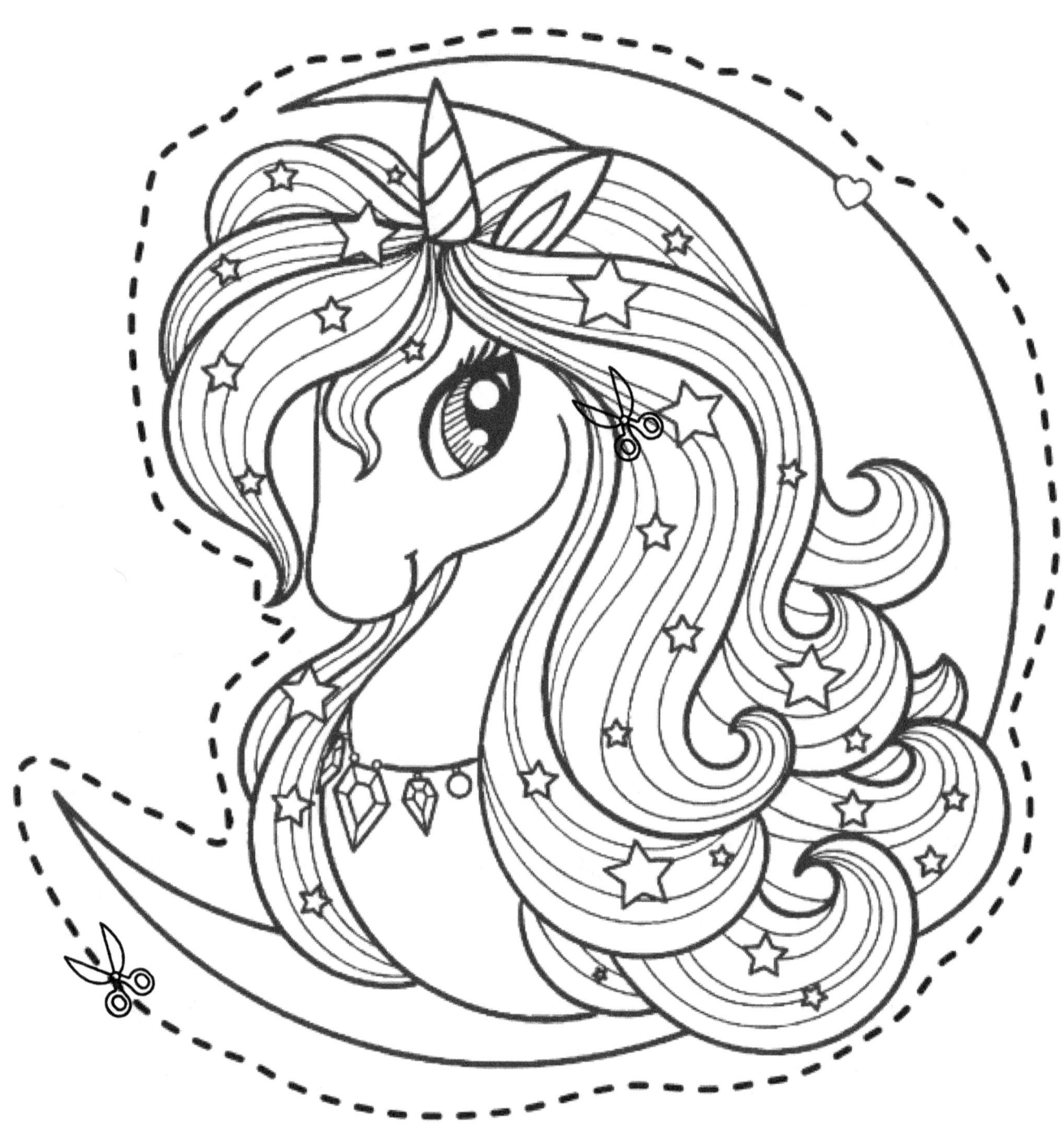

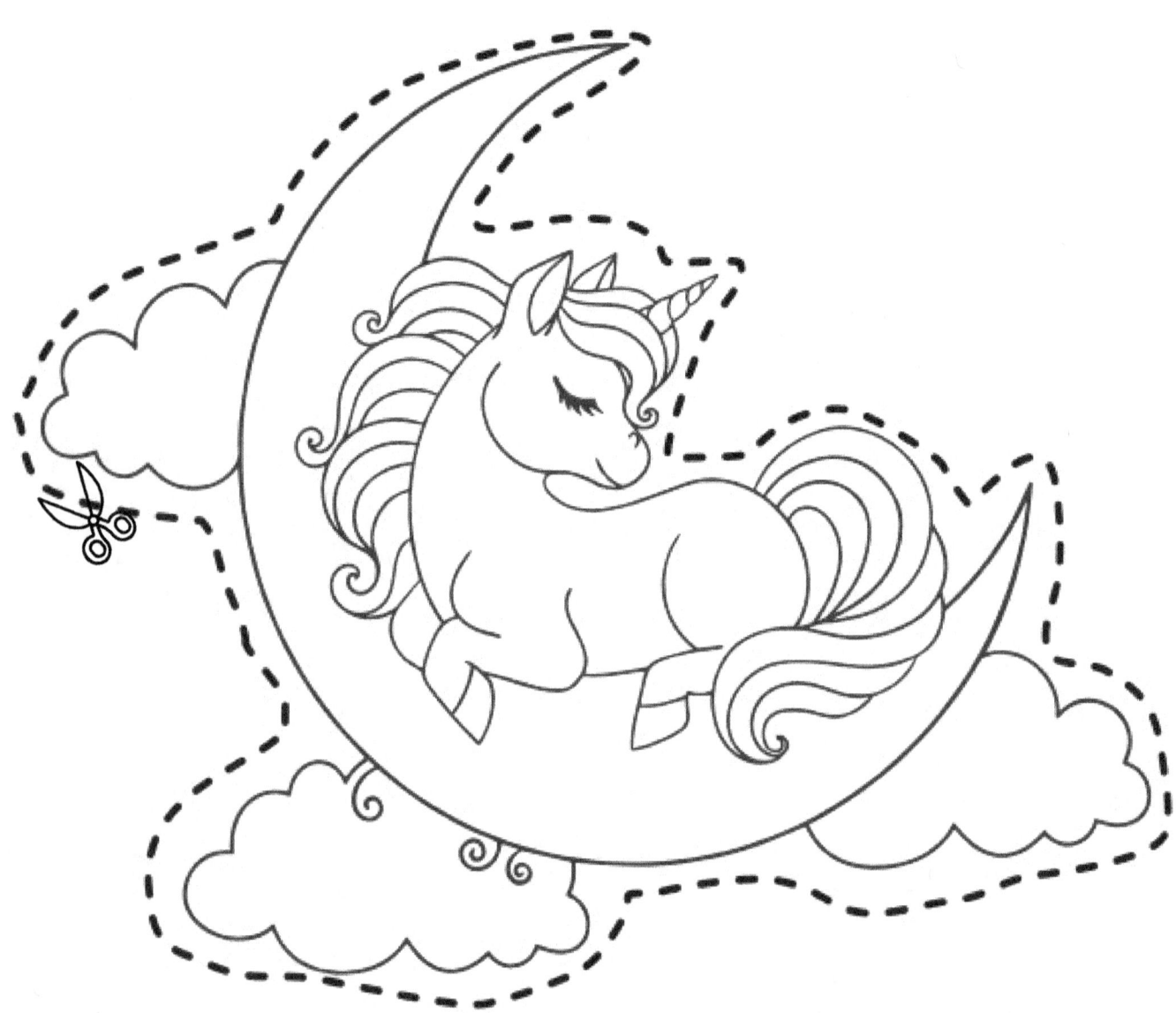

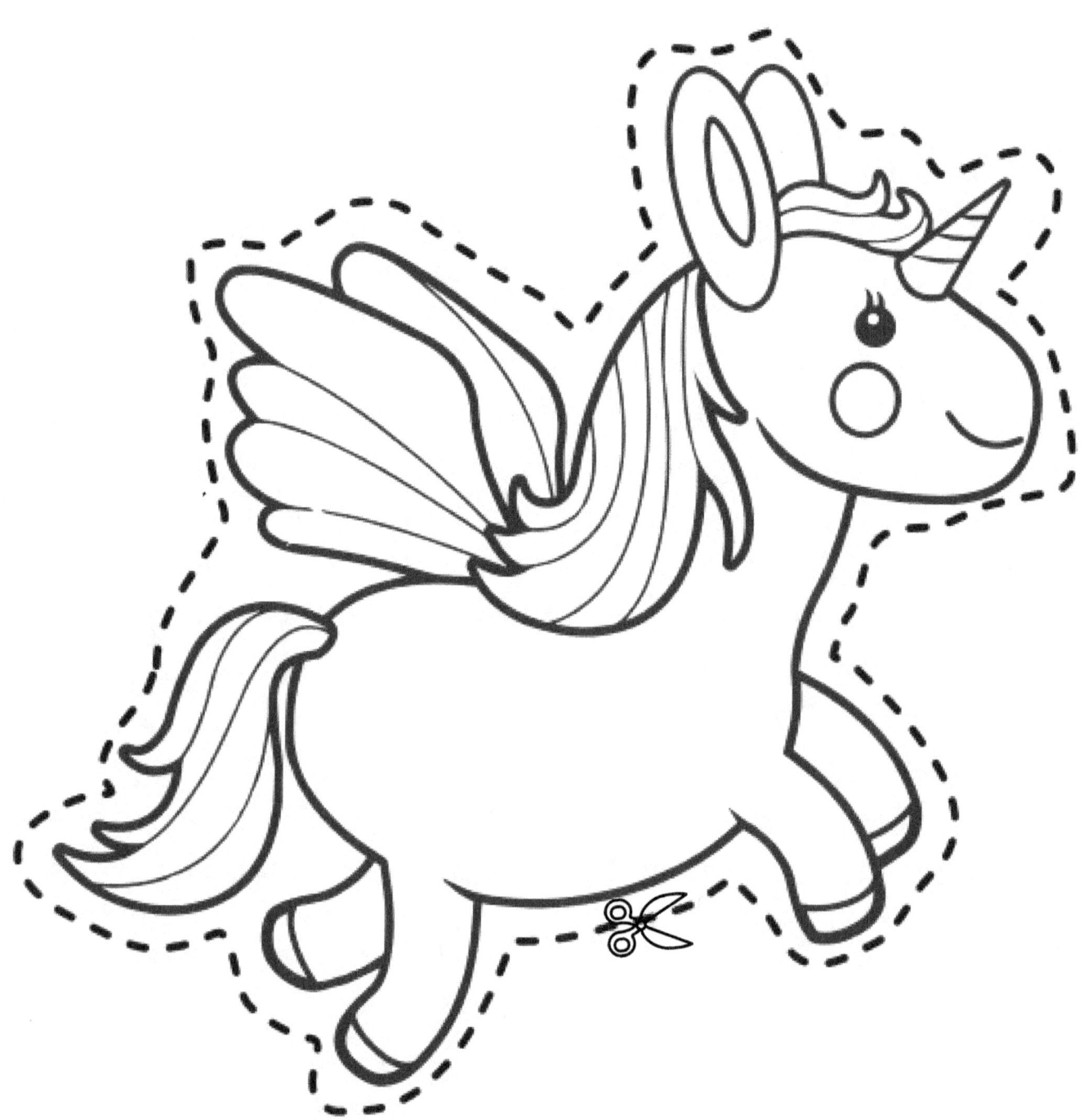

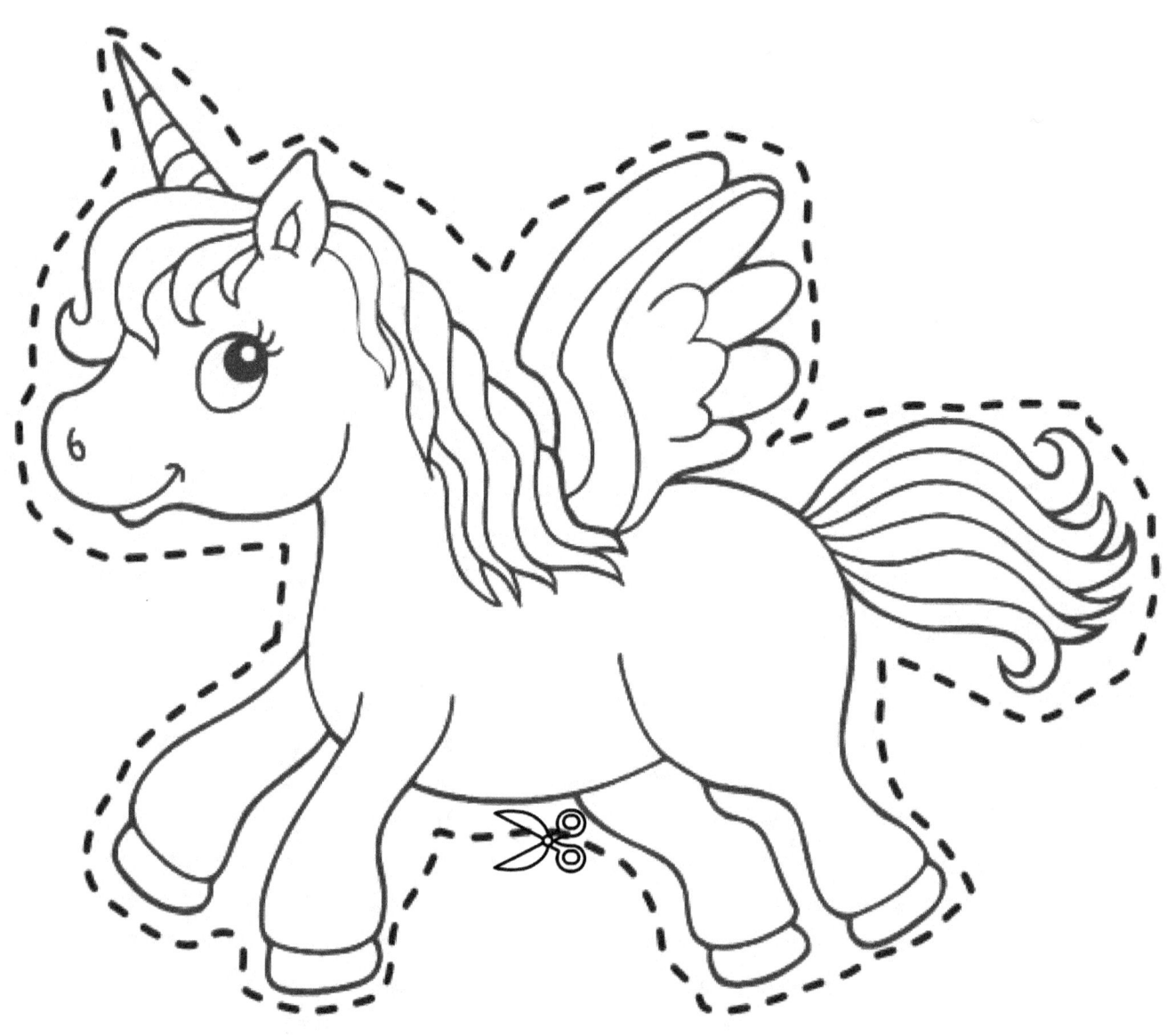

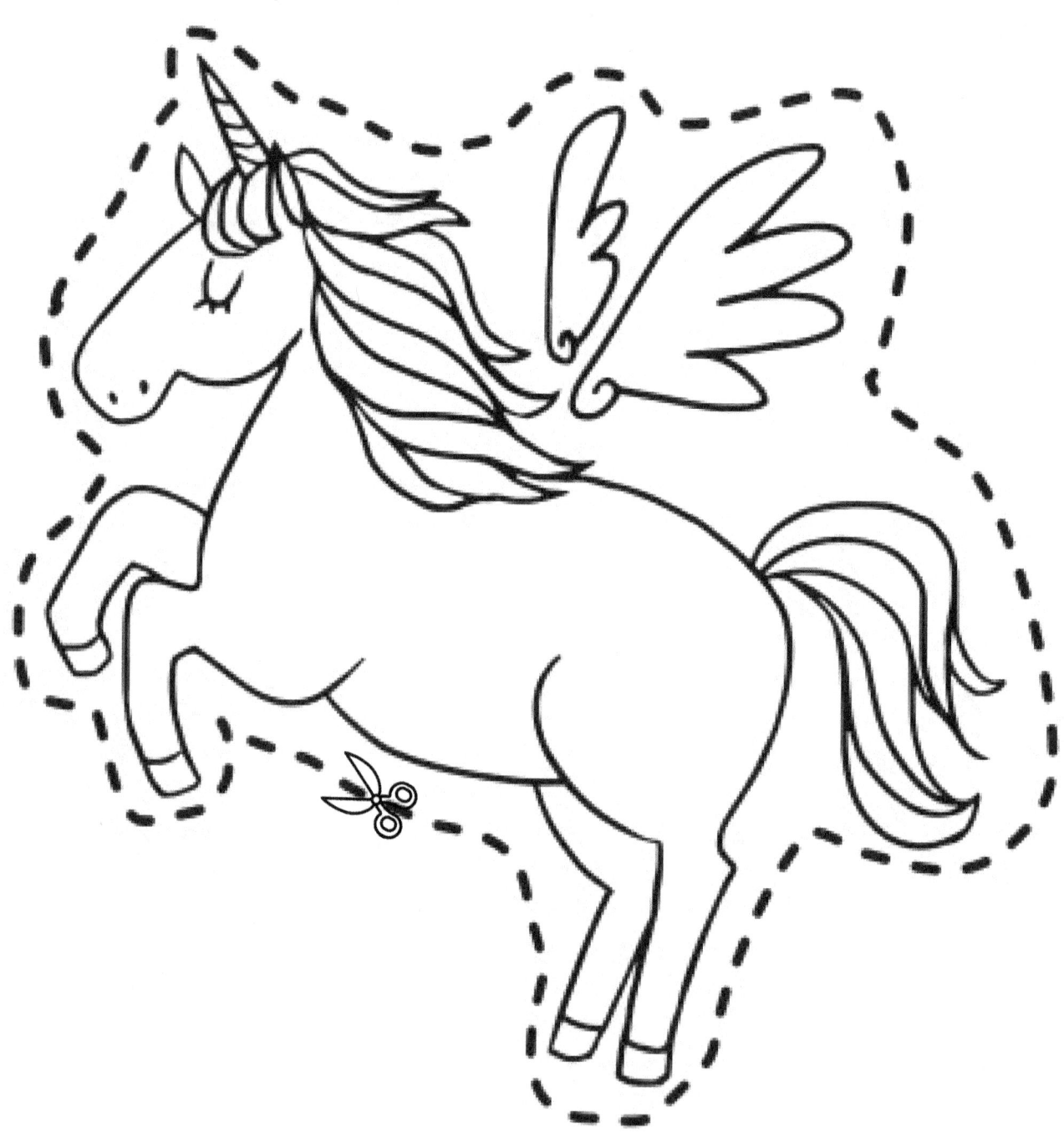

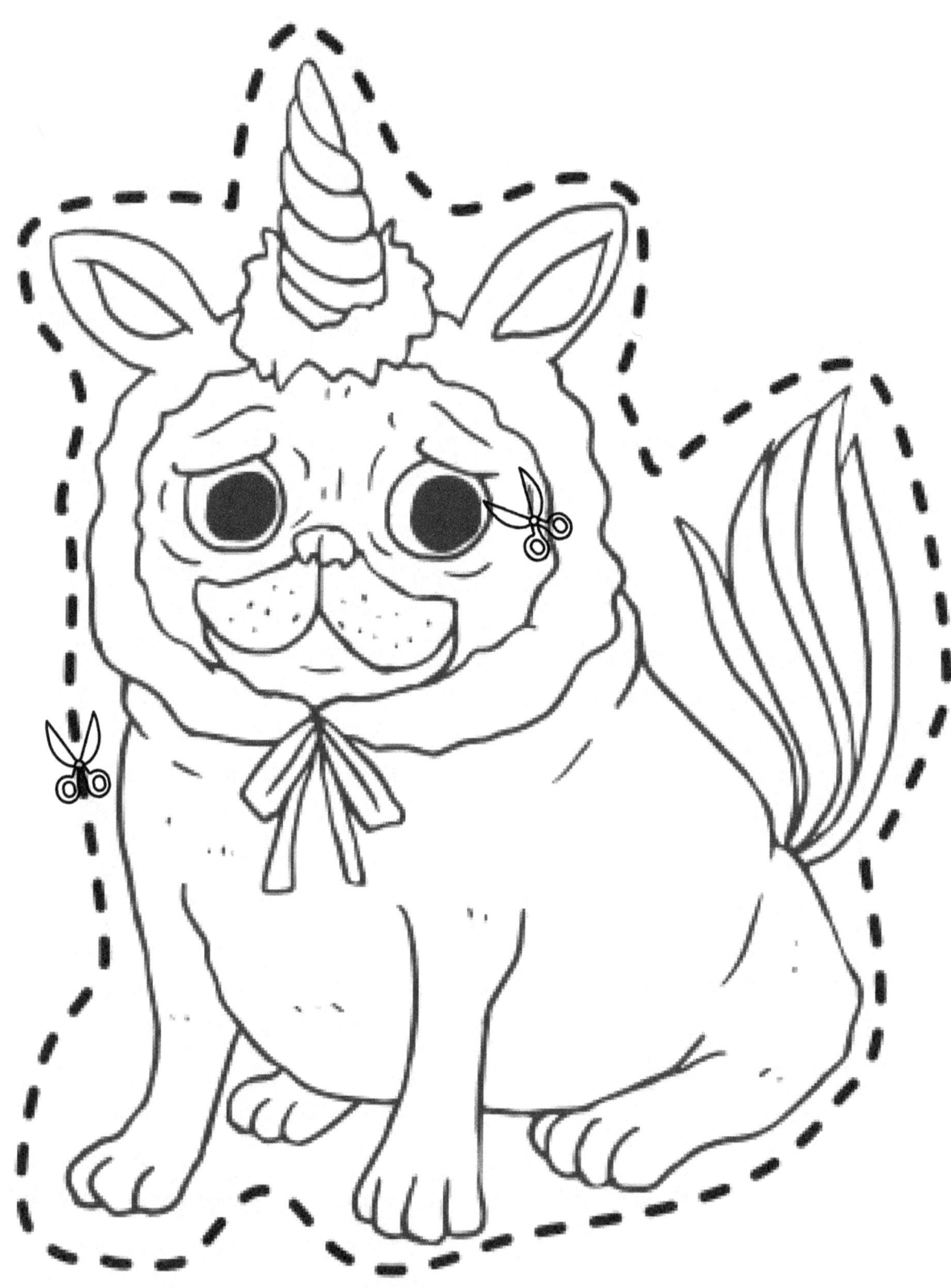

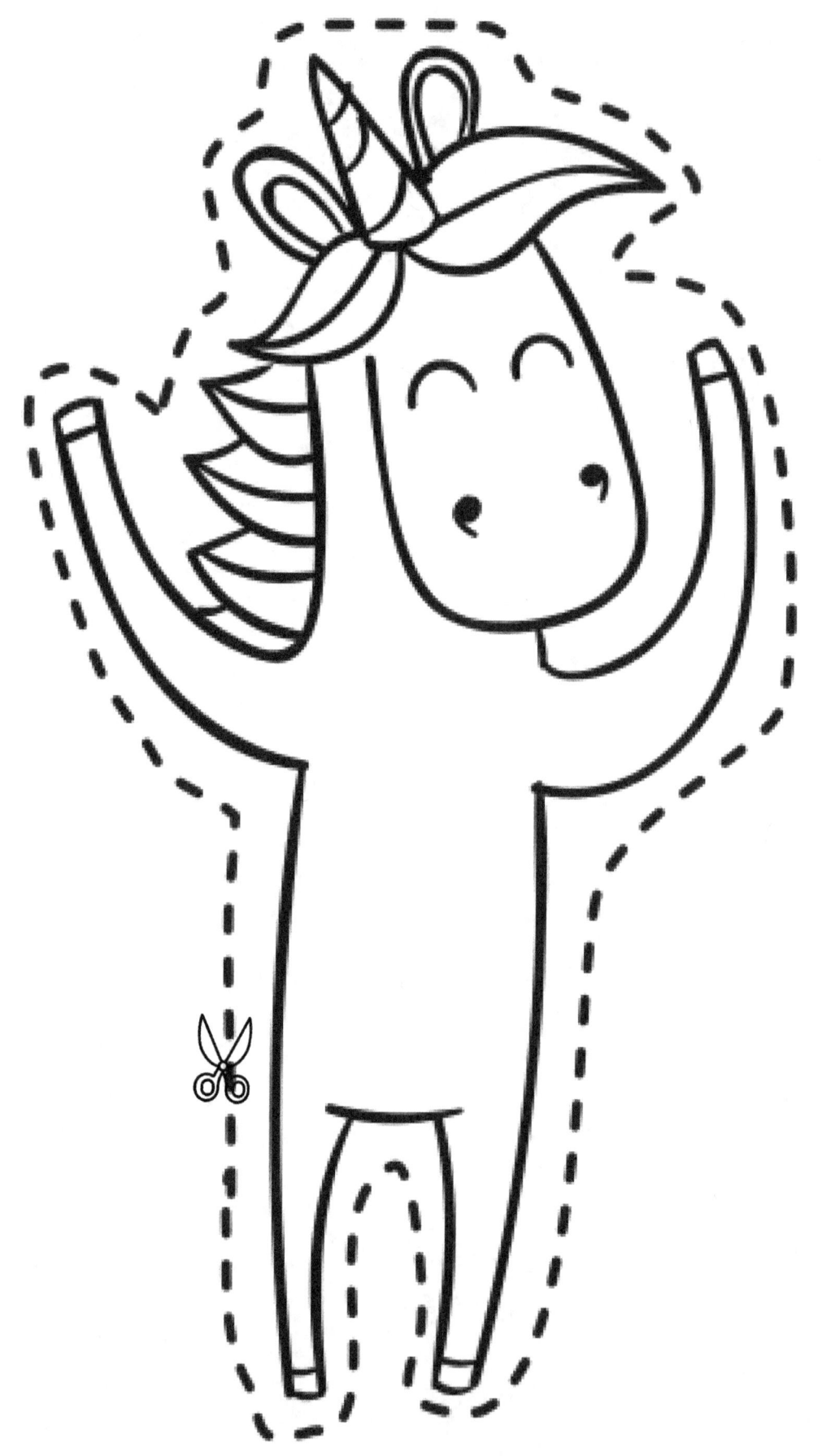

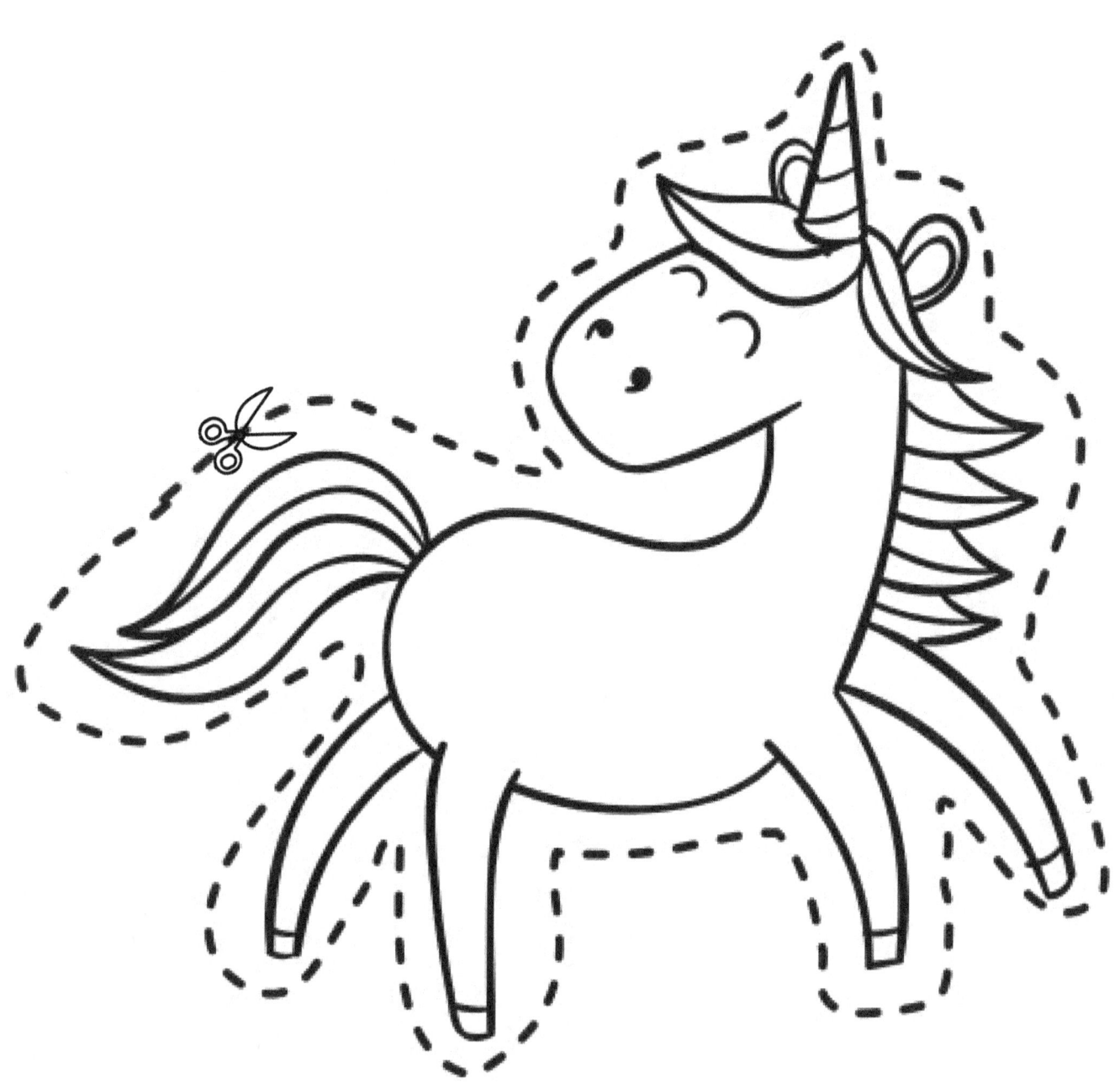

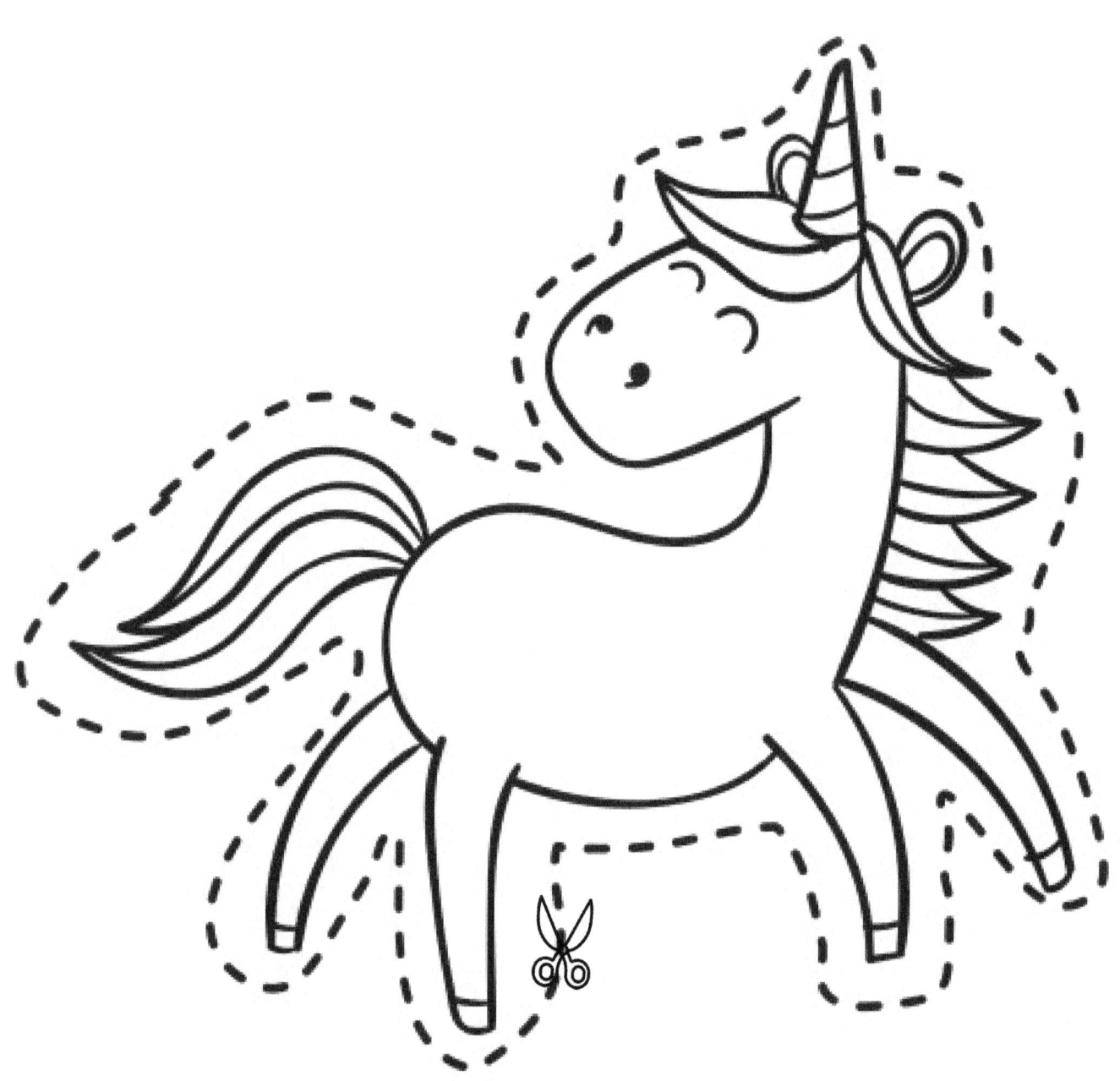